ELMO

This book is brought to you by
the letter M and the number 10!

Illustrated by Art Mawhinney
Cover illustration by DiCicco Studios
Written by Catherine McCafferty
and Brooke Zimmerman

Published by
Louis Weber, C.E.O., Publications International, Ltd.
7373 North Cicero Avenue, Lincolnwood, Illinois 60712

Ground Floor, 59 Gloucester Place, London W1U 8JJ

Customer Service: 1-800-595-8484 or
customer_service@pilbooks.com

www.pilbooks.com

8 7 6 5 4 3 2 1

ISBN-13: 978-1-4127-6987-7
ISBN-10: 1-4127-6987-6

 publications international, ltd.

One bright, sunny morning on Sesame Street, Elmo heard a toe-tapping kind of music. Maybe it was coming from a toy in his toy box!

Can you help Elmo find the letter M, the number 10, and toys that make music?

10
The number 10

M
M is for MUSIC!

toy piano

trumpet

cymbals

tambourine

ukulele

drum

The music was coming from outside! There, children and monsters were playing and singing. They were making music, but it wasn't the same.

Elmo noticed things with strings. Can you spot them, too?

There are 10 yo-yos. Can you find all 10?

M is for marionette

clothesline

kite

paddleball

ball of yarn

Elmo thought he heard some more music coming from Hooper's Store. But it was not the same sound Elmo had heard earlier that morning.

Look around the crowd to find:

Bert and the number 10

M is for music box

The Count

Baby Bear

Betty Lou

Cookie Monster

Rosita

Grover

As Elmo walked down Sesame Street he heard some terrible crashing and banging sounds. It was Oscar the Grouch and his all-Grouch band!

Oscar's trash may look like junk, but to Oscar, it's treasure. Can you find these items?

There are 10 tin cans. Can you find all 10?

M is for milk

racket

shoe

tire

lamp

pillow

Elmo followed more music to 123 Sesame Street, where Ernie was singing to Rubber Duckie. It's fun to make music and bubbles at bathtime!

Lots of duckie friends are there! Can you find these?

There are 10 baby duckies. Can you find all 10?

M is for mop

Trucker Duckie

Lucky Duckie

Grubby Duckie

Duckleberry Swim

Bubble Duckie

Construction Duckie

Elmo began to wonder if he would ever find the music he'd heard before. So he asked Big Bird for help. Big Bird was listening to his favorite kind of music: bird songs!

Can you find these feathered friends?

10 baby birds in 1 nest

M is for mockingbird

Little Bird

early bird

lovebirds

catbird

blue bird

birdbrain

Maybe someone at the park would know where the mystery music was coming from. Elmo headed that way, but a traffic jam of ice cream trucks stopped him in his tracks.

Look around for these yummy frozen treats:

There are 10 ice pops. Can you find all 10?

M is for mint ice cream

ice cream sandwich

twist cone

snow cone

strawberry sundae

banana split

But wait! There was music coming from the park!

Elmo had found the toe-tapping tune he had been looking and listening for all day! Look around and find all 10 "M" bands!

moo band

monster band

mouse band

mandolin band

moose band

monkey band

mermaid band

marching band

magician band

mariachi band

Looking in his toy box made Elmo want to play. Should he play music? Or a sport? Go back to Elmo's room and find these fun, sporty toys. Let's play!

baseball

football

baseball bat

soccer ball

Let's have fun playing and singing outside. Can you find the things the children and monsters are singing about?

I'm a Little **Teapot**

Mary Had a Little **Lamb**

There's a Hole in My **Bucket**

Duckies are just one kind of bird that likes water. Go back to Ernie's bathroom and find these other water-loving birds:

swan

flamingo

pelican

Birds aren't the only things that fly. If you buzz back to Big Bird's nest, you're bound to find these bugs:

bees

butterfly

beetle

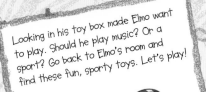

Bert is buying paper clips for 10¢ at Hooper's Store. Can you find these other super-sale prices?

5¢ 50¢
75¢ 25¢

Oscar thinks all his trash is treasure. Can you look through the junk to find some pieces of **real** treasure?

ring

coin

crown

Fruity flavors are delicious. Go back to the playground and find:

grapes

pineapple

banana

apple

When it comes to music, listening is lovely. But dancing is divine! Can you find these three happy dancers in the park?